PRISSY:
A Cat's Tale

Story by **JAN KINSMAN** and **LOUISE HOGAN**

Illustrations by **LOUISE HOGAN**

AuthorHouse™ LLC
1663 Liberty Drive
Bloomington, IN 47403
www.authorhouse.com
Phone: 1-800-839-8640

Illustrations by Louise Hogan

Published by AuthorHouse 07/22/2015

ISBN: 978-1-4918-0908-2(sc)
ISBN: 978-1-4918-0909-9 (e)

Library of Congress Control Number: 2013914702

Any people depicted in stock imagery provided by Thinkstock are models,
and such images are being used for illustrative purposes only.
Certain stock imagery © Thinkstock.

This book is printed on acid-free paper.

author**HOUSE**®

ABOUT THE AUTHOR

She has a compassion for taking care of stray cats, as well as her own cats, and has devoted her time and efforts to do so. She has been rewarded with their love, trust, and affection. Without the help of her co-author, Louise Hogan, her aunt, the book about Prissy would not have been published. Her husband, Joseph, encouraged her to complete the book. He knew how much it meant to her to write about the true life adventures of this wonderful cat.

CO-AUTHOR AND ILLUSTRATOR:

She worked in the banking industry for fifty years and is now retired. She began drawing these unusual facial figures when her husband was very sick. Her friends tell her that these figure drawings were unlike any drawings, they had ever seen before. Without a doubt, her ability to draw these figures came from God.

Philippians 4:13. I can do all things through Christ which strengtheneth me.

My name is Prissy. Meet my friend Hobo. Pete and Tigger are my brothers, and Speckles is my sister.

I do not always get along well with my brothers and sister. They like to chase me around the house. "Please, let's go outside where we can chase bugs and butterflies," I beg them.

pete   speckles

Hobo   Tigger

3

My day starts very early. I have been awake for quite a while and ready to play before it gets too hot, before Mom and Dad are awake, and before the paper boy brings the newspaper. I really wanted to go outside, so I began to meow.

Mom jumped out of bed, quickly walked to the back door, and quietly exclaimed, "Prissy, please go out the door! Why are you meowing so loudly this early in the morning? You are going to wake up everyone in the house."

Mom and Dad take good care of me. They let me come in and out of the house when I want to.

I meowed and meowed at the front door. I thought Mom would never hear me. I wanted to come in. At last, she heard me, and the moment she opened the door, I ran really fast in the house to her bedroom, and hid under her bed. This is my favorite hiding place.

Soon, it was time for me to go outside again. I had been under mom's bed for quite some time.

I heard my mom calling me. "Prissy, where are you? You need to go outside."

My friend Hobo asked, "Why are you ignoring Mom?"

"I am just too tired to go outside right now. Maybe she will forget about me," I said to Hobo.

I was hiding under her bed, when mom found me. She picked me up and carried me out the front door. I do need to go outside because I am a CAT, and that is what CATS do.

This time, I went outside to stretch and lie down in the warm sun. With the soft breeze blowing, I could hardly keep my eyes open.

All of a sudden, I heard the back door open. My brothers, Pete and Tigger and my sister, Speckles ran out of the house. They were angry with me, and said I always got special attention from mom and dad. They started chasing me. To get away from them, I ran very fast and jumped over the fence.

Dad has a special desk where I love to sit. I feel close to him when I take cat naps during the day, sleeping on his important papers.

Every day, Dad plays with me and tries to make me tough. But to tell you the truth, I am a very GIRLY, GIRLY cat.

Being the girly, girly cat that I am, I like to go inside mom's closet, take a look at her clothes, and then find a place among her shoes to take another nap.

There is another thing I like to do and that is to get into her shower when the shower door has been left open. Mom does not know this, but I like to chase my tail around and around in the shower. When I get dizzy, I have to stop. What fun!

Mom is very nice. She feeds me, loves me, and gives me special attention every day. I do not like to eat in a crowd and never eat outside. My brothers and sister go running to mom when they hear her tap on their food bowl. Not me. I run towards the bedroom, and she brings my food bowl to me. There, I can eat by myself without anyone brothering me. She knows I am timid. She also knows that after Tigger eats all his food, he wants to eat mine.

I love where I live and can go anywhere outside. My neighbors watch out for my safety. I like to crawl under their cars no matter if the weather is hot or cold.

It is now the end of another day. I hear Mom calling me for supper. She calls and calls.

Finally, I slowly make my way home, stopping once in a while to scratch those pesky little fleas. I prance, stretch, and take my time going home. Mom named me PRISSY because I am a GIRLY, GIRLY cat.

I heard Mom call me again, but I suddenly saw a beautiful butterfly. I started chasing it. The more it flew around, the harder I tried to catch it. It flew over a small creek filled with water. And you guessed it; the butterfly landed in the middle of the creek and so did I.

It had started raining; lightning lit up the sky, and the thunder was loud. The creek was filling up with more water. Every time I got close to the edge of the creek, the current pulled me back. I just knew I was going to drown. I was scared and started meowing very loudly. My strength was almost gone.

Just when I started going down in the water, I looked up and there stood dad. He stepped into the creek, reached down with both hands, and pulled me out of the water. Because I was wet and cold, I began to shiver. Dad cuddled me in his arms and said, "Prissy, you are safe now and you do not need to be afraid any longer."

On the way home, Dad told me how worried Mom had been after she called you and you did not come home. She just knew you were in trouble. She kept looking and looking outside to see if you were on the front porch. Mom pleaded with me and exclaimed, "please find Prissy and bring her home!" Just before I went outside; I looked out the window, and it was still raining, so I put on my hat, raincoat, and rubber boots to go search for you.

Dad also told me that Hobo, Tigger, Pete, and Speckles would be waiting for us when we get home. They were concerned for your safety and wanted me to find you and bring you home.

I knew at that moment, how much my family *LOVED* me.

True to his word; Dad did find me and we are going home.

Everyone at home anxiously waited for Dad to return. Finally, the back door opened, and Dad was holding me in his arms.

My family was so happy and shouted, "Hooray! Hooray! Hooray for Prissy! We will never be mean to Prissy again."

THE END

MY MOM

JUMPING OVER
THE FENCE

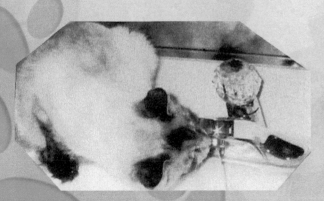

DRINKING WATER
FROM THE SINK

Printed in the United States
by Baker & Taylor Publisher Services